W9-BYH-850

Wannabes

Fashion Queen

Chrysalis Children's Books

★Wannabes★

Fashion Queen

by Moira Butterfield

Chrysalis Children's Books

First published in the UK in 2003 by
⟨⟩ Chrysalis Children's Books,
an imprint of Chrysalis Books Group,
The Chrysalis Building,
Bramley Road, London W10 6SP, UK

This edition is distributed in the U.S. by
Publishers Group West.

Copyright © Chrysalis Books Group PLC

The right of Moira Butterfield to be identified as
the author of this work has been asserted by her
in accordance with the Copyright, Designs and
Patents Act 1988

All rights reserved. No part of this book may
be reproduced or utilized in any form or by any
means, electronic or mechanical, including
photocopying, recording or by any information
storage and retrieval system, without
permission in writing from the publisher except
by a reviewer who may quote brief passages
in a review.

All characters in this book are fictitious and any
resemblance to real persons, living or dead, is
purely coincidental.

British Library Cataloguing in Publication Data
for this book is available from the British Library.

ISBN: 1 844580 48 2

Printed and bound in Great Britain
by Mackays of Chatham plc

Contents

Hi,

I'm Lulu and I LOVE fashion, don't you? I'm going to help make you a fashion expert, just like me! Maybe one day you'll even make to a successful career as a top fashion designer. I say,

"GO GIRL!"

The fun starts here. Soon you'll be dripping with style, and oozing with fashion class!

Good luck, wannabes!

Love from

Lulu B

Chapter 1

Fashion Nightmares...

We all do it sometimes... I'm talking about that one awful mistake that ruins a perfectly good outfit. Yes, it has even happened to me. Come close and I'll tell you a mega secret...

I once wore high-heeled peep-toe shoes with knee-length socks. Well, I **was** only 15 at the time, but the memory still haunts me!

My friends say I'm obsessed with fashion. Moi? I think it was my friend Sally who first said I'm fashion-fixated, but I stopped listening to her when I realized she was wearing scuffed shoes. Someone else said I was a fashion victim. I didn't pay any attention to her because she was wearing green... (Sooo last year.)

Anyway, my point is that things do go wrong, even for the super-stylish. Did you know that International supermodel Naomi Campbell once fell off some high platform shoes right in the

middle of a Paris fashion show? I would have caught her but I was wearing linen, and it creases so easily.

Oh, all right, I admit it. I love clothes. But that makes me the best person to help you become style superstars.

Anyway, those girlfriends are just so wrong about me. I'm not totally obsessed by fashion...ooh, I'm about to go over to the next page. I think that calls for a new outfit...

THINGS TO DO

Must send friends my top ten fashion disasters and invite them to my house for a makeover party.

So where was I? Oh yes, fashion is such a tricky business, full of trend traps and style pitfalls, so you're lucky I'm here to guide you through to dazzling clothes perfection. But first I have to warn you: DON'T MAKE FASHION ENEMIES! We all need fashion tips sometimes, don't we? We rely on our friends to tell us what looks good and what we should recycle as a polishing rag, but I've learned there are ways to say, "you look like garbage," without hurting feelings. When you see a friend in need of fashion-doctoring, always remember Lulu's "let-down lightly" tips. Never say: "You're so brave to wear that!" or "Aren't you going to change?" Instead, say: "You look great, but you'd look absolutely perfect if..."

Don't lose friends because of fashion. You never know when you'll need them to tell you that your dress is tucked in your drawers!

WARNING!

Top Ten Fashion Disasters!

The next few pages could cause fashion fans great distress.

I can't possibly tell you who I've seen wearing these terrible mistakes. That would be revealing too much of the awful truth. Let's just say the guilty KNOW who they are!

If you want to be a fashion success, never, never get caught showing one of these...

Underwear Shame!

1 Big Pants
Old underwear showing over your pants when you bend over.

2 Double Rear
Caused by too-tight underwear.

3 V.P.L
Visible pantie line.
EEEK!

4 Workman's Rear
Showing more than you should at the back.

5 Underarm Plague!

White lines caused by dressing before your deodorant is dry.

6 Button Explosion

RUN! That button's going to ping off any second now!

7 Oldie Dressing

Dressing like an older, more practical, but more BORING generation.

8 Unidentified Stains

Sorry, our artist could not draw these, as it was just too upsetting.

9 Sock Horror

Long thick socks with sandles. Only someone very sick and cruel would do this to the world.

Your own personal fashion hatred

The awful sight that fills you with the most style horror.

Chapter 2

Create Your Own Style

Fashion is all about putting together a style that says something about you. Whatever you wear, you'll be silently sending powerful messages to everyone who sees you. I'm told that my clothes simply scream "fashion queen," along with "so now!" and "hot!"

I went out and spoke to people about their style today. Once they'd got over the thrill of meeting me we discussed the messages their clothes were sending to the world.

The first woman I saw was wearing black jeans, a "rock on" t-shirt, and a leather jacket, with her hair in a ponytail. "Did you know that your clothes message today is 'Don't mess with me. I'm a tough woman'?" I remarked. "That's not good. I'm a guy," he said. Oops! Bad start!

Then someone flagged me down in my car. Fans, fans everywhere! This one was wearing a snappy uniform look, which said: "I'm in control." She turned out to be a traffic speed cop. So I was absolutely right, wasn't I? Later I met my friend Ellie, a real campaigner with a head full of politics. She was excited about two new campaigns she was running: Save the Dingbat; and Eat Planet-friendly Cookies. She was showing them on her clothes, with a slogan t-shirt and lots of campaign buttons. Good for her. She's using her style to tell the world what she thinks, and you can avoid her if you don't agree and think she's a dingbat herself.

When you get up in the morning, your first thought should be: "What subtle psychological message do I want to convey with my clothes today?" or, to put it more simply: "What do I feel like wearing?" If your answer to that is "Whatever's lying around on the floor will be fine," then shame, shame, shame on you! Write a hundred punishment lines: "I must listen to Lulu."

To get a style grip on your life, keep this book beside your bed and read it thoroughly day and night until your style message comes across strongly to everyone with the unmistakable vibe: "I'm gorgeous!"

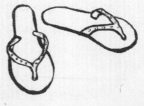

Do You Need a Style Guru?

Are you a style superstar or have you lost your fashion groove? Take my test to find out just how much help you're going to need.

1. You are invited to give a speech at a big conference. Which outfit would you wear?

a A smart suit to look important.
b A strap dress to look glamorous.
c Combat trousers to feel comfortable.

2. You're going on a beach holiday. What useful item would you buy at the airport?

a Bikini   **b** Nightgown   **c** Chocolate bar

3. You are going to a smart wedding. Which hat would you wear?

a An elegant straw hat.
b An arty hat that you have made yourself.
c A baseball cap.

4. Which of these fashion sayings would you agree with?

a "You can never own too many shoes, darling."
b "Red with green should never be seen."
c "Grannie always knows best."

5. How often do you buy new underwear?

a Very regularly.
b When the old ones turn gray and baggy.
c You didn't know stores sold underwear.

6. How often do you buy fashion magazines?

a All the time.
b Occasionally.
c Never. You only read the free ones in the dentist's waiting room.

7. Which of these compliments do you get the most?

a "You look great."
b "You look well."
c "You look...different."

Mostly a's

You've got it, girl! Style runs in your fashionably red blood. Use your talent to make it to the top of the chic designer ladder.

Mostly b's

Like so many, your style sense is patchy and goes up and down like a saggy pair of socks. Read this book to improve your chances of super-styledom.

Mostly c's

Let's face it. At the moment you have the style-sense of a geeky granddad. You need help! Study this book from dawn till dusk, or stay stuck forever in a fashion nightmare.

SOS Star Rescue

Celebrities call me day and night for advice on what to wear. I have set up a fashion advice emergency helpline for the poor dears. Here are today's messages:

A VERY famous football player rang. His team's new away strip doesn't suit him. My advice: How terrible! Get a transfer right away!

A TERRIBLY famous popstar rang. He wants to wear very tight pants on stage but they show his underwear lines. My advice: Wear a thong for the song, dahling.

A TOP celebrity is going on holiday and wants something that looks good wet and dry. I say... we were not meant to get wet unless it's at a luxury spa!

Do you know any style-free celebrities that look awful? Send them my SOS STAR RESCUE kit. It contains my autographed photo, helpline number, and a large paper bag with eye holes, for days when they're looking really grungy.

Style Emergency

Use my fashion speak to get out of trouble instantly.

Broken zipper?

"It's designer grunge, darling."

Someone wearing the same outfit as you at a party?

"Ah, but mine fits."

Run in your hose?

"I'm making a protest against boring perfection."

Ketchup splattered on you?

"It's art."

Heel breaks?

"I'm auditioning for a part with a limp."

Your Style Read-Out

I was born with style. I would only play with designer baby rattles and use color-coordinated diapers. If you need a little more help, you could try matching your clothes to your personality. Look at each box and decide which statements are true for you. Put a checkmark beside those that apply to you.

Type a

You like performing

You like glittery things

You sometimes have a fiery temper

You are generous

You don't like being alone for long

You gesture a lot when you speak

You sometimes sulk when you don't get your way

Type b

You like a challenge

You never give up

You get bored quickly

You are practical

You like sports

You are sometimes quiet

You get dressed quickly in the morning

Type c

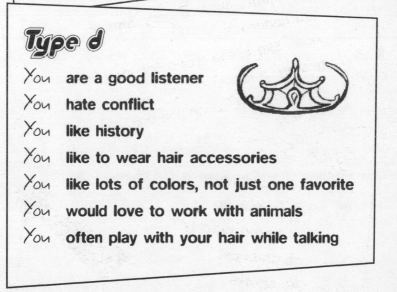

You are sometimes impatient

You have an independent streak

You speak up if you think something is unjust

You are very loyal to your friends

You often point a finger when you speak

You like dramatic-looking jewelry

Type d

You are a good listener

You hate conflict

You like history

You like to wear hair accessories

You like lots of colors, not just one favorite

You would love to work with animals

You often play with your hair while talking

Mostly Type a ticks

You are a glam girl. Your ideal look is a glitzy, film-star style that looks very expensive. Think Oscars, theater premieres, red carpets, and limos.

Shopping words: glitter, pink, straps, glitter, jewels, glitter.

Mostly Type b ticks

You are an adventure girl, the kind who might trek up a mountain, bungee-jump, or play in a game of sports, all on the same day if possible. Dress like Lara Croft or an athlete.

Shopping words: combats, trainers, tracksuits, numbers, sports teams.

Mostly Type c ticks

You are a goth girl. Think black with a touch of red. Think leather and lace. Watch out, Buffy; there's a touch of the vampire about you. You belong in art school.

Shopping words:: black, red, spiky jewelry, biker girl, drama.

Mostly Type d ticks

You are a hippie girl. You feel empathy with swirly, long skirts teamed with peasant tops and ethnic everything. Aim for a slight grunge effect (but please don't forget to wash).

Shopping words: ethnic, tie-dye, long-length, toe rings, fake flower tattoos.

Checks all over the place

Fashion magpie. Try all of the looks, but not all together, or you could end up looking like a scary split personality.

Set Your Own Trend

A celebrity can start a worldwide fashion trend by wearing something fab in a video or movie, or on an album cover. I've started many trends myself by appearing at events in something original that becomes instantly popular. Wouldn't it be fun to start your own trend? Here are some ideas you could try.

The in-crowd route

Give all your coolest friends your chosen trend item as a present. Then watch as the style spreads like a fashion rash.

The TV weirdo route

Only try this if your trend idea looks really odd and surprising—wearing vegetables, for example, or painting your cheeks purple. Get yourself on TV,

THINGS TO DO

Buy a new closet. Do they make "truck-size," I wonder?

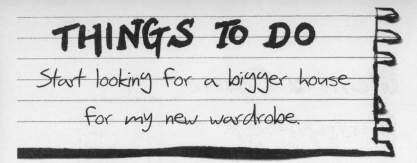

THINGS TO DO

Start looking for a bigger house for my new wardrobe.

ideally one of those Saturday morning shows with kids in the audience. They're bound to pick you out of the crowd. Make sure you give the program presenters your trendy item to try (a gift of purple face paint, carrot earrings, or whatever).

The mobile route

Text message everyone you know to convince them of your new trend. Here's an example.

`:-)! WC!

Translation: one eyebrow shaved off!
Way cool!

The career move

Big fashion companies employ people who trawl the planet looking for hot teenage trends and cool stuff to sell. They help set the fashion agenda for the rest of us. It sounds like fashion heaven.

This may take a little longer...

Become a worldwide star. Then whatever you wear will be copied, even carrot earrings.

Wanna Come Shopping?

Are you a shopaholic? Do you personally check every rail of every clothes shop in town, on a regular basis, or do you hate the whole sweaty, crowded business?

I must say, I usually love it, but there are times—even for a fashion queen like me—when it's a strain. You know the scenario—you find something yummy but it's not on the rail in your size, or it has a broken zipper, or the line for the changing rooms looks like a record-attempt for the world's longest bore fest.

I can't prevent all that, but my advice is to treat clothes shopping like a military operation. Make a top-secret mission plan before you go (you could call it a shopping list). Then think yourself into the part of a highly trained shopping-soldier. Zone in on your target shops one by one, with the cool-as-a-cucumber style of a true professional, never losing your control. Get that little top or that new skirt in your sights and swoop.

Check you have this **Vital Mission Equipment** before you go on a shopping expedition:

1 Money

2 Purse

3 Comfortable shoes

4 Map of suitable cafés for regular chocolate cookie fill-ups during mission.

Oh, and one more warning. It's fun to shop with friends, but never go shopping with someone who is not in the mood, who isn't interested in fashion, or who will say irritating things like:

"Why do you want that, for goodness sake?" or

"How many shoes do you actually need to see before you decide?"

Of course, your parents may say these things when out shopping with you, but you will have to grit your teeth with them as they are often in charge of **Vital Mission Equipment number 1**.

☆ **Designer obsessive's shopping list for a party outfit** ☆

Gucci shoes—diamante straps, small heel in gold or silver?

Tiffany jewelry—dramatic diamonds—earrings, necklace, bracelet to match shoes.

Versace gown—shiny, straps, as many sequins as possible.

Clutch bag—no bigger than my cellphone—sequinned, gold clasp.

SHOPPING HATER'S SHOPPING LIST FOR A PARTY OUTFIT

Some sort of
top thing
Cookies

Chapter 3

Planet Fashion

Probably you're wondering what a fashion queen does between shopping and changing outfits. Admittedly there's not much time for serious fun, as I have so many duties and I can't let my friends down. Here's a typical week…

Monday

I jet over to New York to see an exclusive couture collection. Funky ripped leggings and fur-trimmed shorts. Will they catch on? It's up to me. If I wear them, they almost certainly will.

Tuesday

My friends from **Look Good** beg me to help out at a photography session for winter clothing. Fake snow and husky dogs. A dog chews a $500 shoe, but luckily the teeth-marks look divine.

Wednesday

I do the fashion styling on a boy band video. Combats, hoods, and four buckets of hair gel.

Thursday

I meet celebrity photographer David Latchkey at his exhibition. He autographs my book and I autograph his camera case.

Friday

Today I am going to be interviewed about my new book. What shall I wear? Black, I think.

Saturday

Having a few celebrity friends to my place for a style makeover (see page 57). Better make sure I have enough macrobiotic nibbles and put out the yoga mats.

Sunday

Style makeover went very well but my chums have "borrowed" all my favorite clothes… so I'm going shopping for some replacement outfits.

Whatever I'm doing, I have to look great. How do I cope? With black, of course. At all occasions fashion insiders always wear black. Dull? I prefer to call it sophisticated. Now where is that black dye?

Lulu, always a pleasure to work with you, darling.

Mwa Mwa X X

Dave

Fashion Speak

Gaultier or Versace?

All fashion wannabes should drop these words into their everyday conversation – especially when out shopping:

Couture ─────────────

Hand-made pieces of clothing, personally designed and made especially for one client (a very rich one). Couture clothes cost a lot of money because of the time and skill it takes to make them. A suit might take about 200 hours, with client fittings, discussions about fabrics etc, and the very best tailoring. The top couture companies are called "fashion houses." They include such famous names as Chanel, Dior, and Versace.

Ready made ─────────────

Clothes that are mass-made in a factory, copying a designer's original sketches. They're the kind of clothes you buy in chain stores. They are made in big quantities, using machine-stitching and less expensive fabrics than a couturier would choose. That's why a ready-made outfit is much cheaper than a couture item. Ready-made fashion companies have their own brand names, called "labels," such as Diesel or Levi's.

Rag trade

The fashion business.

High Street

Popular ready-made fashion sold everywhere.

THINGS TO DO

Reply to invitation to see
  Milan collections.

Yes please!

Buy more black.

Ask Me Anything, Sweetie!

I'm always being asked for interviews. This is a copy of the interview I did to publicize my new book. Who knows? One day, my life might be filmed—**Woman in Black** would be a good movie title, I think.

Interviewer: **Lulu, it's a pleasure to meet you. Tell me about your new book. Did you really write it all yourself?**

Lulu: Just a minute. Are those novelty cartoon socks you're wearing?

Interviewer: **Yes, do you like them? I thought they looked fun.**

Lulu: Excuse me. I'm feeling sick.

Interviewer: **Are you all right now? What? You want me to take off my socks? Well, OK.... Now, your book is all about how to look great. You always look gorgeous, of course. What's your style secret, Lulu?**

Lulu: Yes, my secret... Look, before we go on can I ask you about your suit. Is it very old?

Interviewer: Er, well...

Lulu: You really should try one of the new suit styles, and I think you'd look great in a Gaultier-label kilt.

Interviewer: Hmm. Lulu, do you ever stop thinking about fashion?

Lulu: Of course I do—when I'm asleep, although come to think of it, I did dream about sleeves last night.

Interviewer: Gosh, I wonder if you'll dream about my suit tonight?

Lulu: That would be a nightmare, darling.

Interviewer: Is fashion so very important?

Lulu: Oh yes. Imagine no fashion! We'd all be wearing horrible animal skins like cave people, although I've heard the caveman look will be back soon. Book in for long hair extensions and keep watch for fake fur.

Interviewer: Who, me?

Lulu: Yes, you. Now put away that silly tape recorder. We're going shopping.

Who Does What in Fashion

I am not known as the Fashion Queen for nothing. I can write about fashion, photograph it, and of course, wear it. But you can always specialize in one area. These are the specialists who help to make my life a lot easier:

Stylist

A practical hard-worker who also has lots of flair. They must put together all the extras a model needs for a photo shoot or a show, from shoes and jewelry to the right makeup and hairstyle.

Head tailor

A perfectionist with patience mixed in. Able to translate your incredibly fabulous ideas into beautifully made clothes, and never bat an eyelid when asked to work on ever-weirder creations.

Photographer

Able to set up magazine publicity shots of your work with stylish pizzazz. Must be able to order models around without upsetting them. A big flamboyant personality would help get more publicity for your clothes.

PR person

A thorough, persistent person who won't take no for an answer. Must send out invitations for shows and launch parties to all the right people, to make sure you get lots of press coverage for your collection.

Model

An unbelievably beautiful person who doesn't mind being ordered around and made to wear all kinds of weird and wonderful things.

Celebrity friends

Who will be the celebrities who wear your clothes and get you lots of publicity?

From Show to Shop

I always get the latest couture clothes sent for free, but how do a top designer's expensive ideas filter down into ordinary shops? Well, not all of them do. Some are just too wacky. But here's how a popular couture idea finds its way into a chain store.

1. A new couture collection gets shown on the catwalk for the first time. All the top fashion journalists are there, along with the super-rich clients and celebrities.

2. Something really grabs the audience—a type of jacket, say, or a look that the designer has chosen to run through the collection: the "peasant look" or "punk look," for instance.

3. The look is featured in upmarket fashion magazines like **Vogue**.

4. It becomes a trend when stars start to wear it, everyone is talking about it and ready-made clothing companies copy the style for main street stores.

Color Vibes

Each new fashion season brings new shows, new collections, new ideas, and one or two must-have colors that everyone decides are "in." Here is my take on the language of color selection.

Red

Red dye used to be made from the juice of crushed insects. Yeech! Let's move on quickly. Bright red is bold, exciting, and daring. It's the color of emergencies and warnings, so it gets you noticed. Red is good for glamor dresses.

Yellow

A sunny, happy color, but when it's bright, it's very noticeable. When I think of yellow, I think of sunshine and holidays (preferably on a luxury yacht).

Orange

Orange is tropical, warm, and full of fun. It's very attention-seeking, so of course I love it! Don't wear too much plain orange at the same time. You'll end up looking like a human lollipop, which is not good.

Blue

Blue is a calm, cool color. It sometimes symbolizes loyalty, because it's used in uniforms a lot. There are a million different blues to choose from—from baby blue to navy blue (good for that yacht). I have even perfected my own "Lulu blue" for my personal chauffeur's uniform.

Green

Green can be a calm, quiet color that brings to mind birdsong and nature walks, but... flip to zingy tropical lime, and we're talking limbo-dancing, party-partying under the moonlit palm trees in the bay where you've moored your yacht for the night.

Purple

In Ancient Egypt, purple dye used to be made by soaking thousands of snails in liquid (who on earth found out how to do something like that in the first place?). It looks great on ritzy glamor clothes. Add swirls to purple, and you get a hippie-freaky, retro 70s look.

Pink

Another split-personality color. It can be sugary, innocent, babyish... but vivid pink is wild and shocking. Yeah, baby!

White

Symbol of purity, holiness, peace, tennis players, and good washing machines.

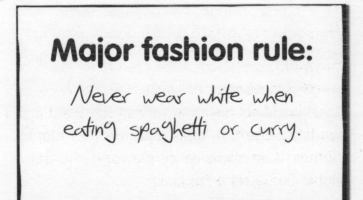

Black

I could mention Halloween—vampires, bats, etc. But I prefer to concentrate on black as the color of simple yet sophisticated style. And it is slimming.

Major fashion rule:

Never wear white when eating spaghetti or curry.

Chapter 4

You Were Wonderful, Darling!

Imagine that you are a famous fashion designer holding a fashion show. Lights are flashing; music is pounding. All heads are turned to the catwalk as impossibly beautiful people begin to parade forward in your new designs. The world's fashion press, its most influential buyers, its most glittering celebrities, and richest fashion clients are all sitting in the front row of the audience. They gasp as each new, stunning outfit comes onstage, and applaud wildly when you came out to take a bow. What a triumph! Kisses and congratulations all around, darling!

But wait, fashion fans. Before you rush off to create your first designs, I must warn you that things don't always go so smoothly. Sometimes the models break down in tears backstage and the clothes don't turn up until the very very last minute, by which time you will have bitten off all your chic nail art. And worst of all, imagine if the invitations go astray and the only person who comes is your aunt. The shame!

In real life, of course, a fashion show is often a mixture of dream and nightmare. Backstage can be frantic, fraught with difficulties and crises, while at the same time, scoring a fantastic success on the catwalk.

A fashion show designer is like a swan on a pond—calm on the surface but paddling like crazy underwater to stay afloat. A catwalk show takes a lot of effort because it's very important. It's the moment when a new collection gets shown for the first time, to the most important people in the business, and there's no guarantee they're going to be nice about it. You just have to put yourself on the line and hope they appreciate your taste and talent. Here are some tips I hope will help if you ever make it to a real catwalk. If you do, make sure you don't forget my invitation!

new talent

fashion week

LULU-front row seat

VIP pass

Do

- Put all the most important people (especially me) in the front row, so they have the best view.

- Give your guests loads of freebies with your name all over them.

- Choose the right music to suit your clothes style. Chillin' or kickin' beats? You must decide.

- Add a few unexpected and original surprises to your collection to wake up your audience—giant hooped pants legs, slashed plastic garbage-can liners, or whatever you want.

- If you throw a tantrum backstage, make it a really worthwhile loud, explosive one. Otherwise, what's the point?

Don't

- Put your models in such high shoes that they fall on to the front row and end up squashing your top guests.

Soooo directional, soooo now!

Fabulous, baby!

- Make a lifelong enemy of a top fashion journalist by giving her a back seat or forgetting to send her an invitation altogether. If you do, you'll soon see why we call it the "cat" walk. Meow! Her claws will come out.

- Forget to praise your hard-working backstage team. Without them, a fashion designer really would wake up screaming.

-Front Row -

The A List: Top buyer, celebrities, and fashion journalists.

-Middle Rows -

Front row's people: Their bodyguards, stylists, assistants, and dog-walkers.

-Back Rows -

Anyone who has been rude to you. Anyone wearing clothes by rival designers.

-XXXXXXX -

To be kept out by your bodyguards: People wearing leggings, golf clothing, or socks with sandals.

Go On, Show Off...

There's no need to leave all the fun to fashion stars like me. Go ahead and have your own fashion show. Hold it in your hallway with a group of hand-picked, trustworthy friends as models and audience combined.

Ask your friends to bring a bagful of their clothes with them (labeled with their names, so that everything doesn't get mixed up). They should each bring four outfits, on four themes that you give them. I suggest:

Summer fun

Crazy clothes

Party!

Winter wonderland

Choose some good music, do each other's hair, and parade your outfits. Get someone to take photographs so you can make your own fashion show album.

The Art Part

Even if you don't want to hold a fashion show, you can still draw and color a clothes collection. Design for me, if you like. I ALWAYS want new outfits. You don't need to be good at drawing figures, which even I find pretty difficult. Instead, do stylized figures that are simple and quick, but show off the shape of the clothes.

Here are some ideas to try:

Really simple elongated face shape

Simple features

Elegant body parts

Long long legs

Elongated arms

Strong lines

What I Say + What I Mean

I hate to be rude about designers.* Between you and me, I don't always say EXACTLY what I mean when I see a new collection.

Me: "The new collection was an interesting mix, using animal inspiration."

Translation: "A gorilla wouldn't be caught in it."

Me: "The clothes had a retro flavor."

Translation: "There were no new ideas."

Me: "The new collection had a dreamy quality."

Translation: "Oops, I fell asleep during the show."

Me: "The designer has been inspired by loose forms."

Translation: "All the clothes looked like old sacks, darling."

* Unless they put me in the back row at their show, in which case they're in BIG trouble.

My Inspiration

Designers and fashion queens usually keep scraps of material they like, plus photos clipped from magazines, and anything else that gives them inspiration. I've made my own ideas board to help inspire you…

Love polka dots today!

Barcode—good on range of t-shirts?

Teabag made me think of scented clothes

flowerpot—excellent shape for a hat

Magazine Madness

Look Good magazine begged me to be their guest editor for a month, and knowing you would love to know what goes on at the offices of a fashion magazine, I agreed. Here is my diary of the run-up to the new edition.

Planning meeting ─────

The next edition has to have a theme, but what? Suggestions include black, brown (the new black), underwater clothes, retro (same as last month), vegetable jewelry or the peasant look. I decide on the peasant look. Someone suggests using a donkey in the fashion photo shoot.

Location ─────

Where will the photo shoot be? A mountain village? A farm? We decide on the Caribbean—far away, but soooo warm at this time of year.

The magazine accountant cancels the Caribbean trip. Such a spoilsport. We will do the shoot in a local studio instead. I choose David Latchkey as the photographer, plus top model, Tikitta. They are both thrilled to work with me.

Day of the shoot ──────────

The donkey arrives. Sweet!

Tikitta gets her hair done by the stylist to look like a peasant who doesn't own a hairbrush. The "simple girl peasant" makeup takes two hours. The donkey becomes bored and starts to act up.

Dave throws a tantrum because Tikitta yawns during a shot.

Tikitta throws a tantrum because the stylist spends more time making up the donkey than she does on Tikitta.

The donkey throws a tantrum. Nobody knows why.

Six hours and hundreds of photos later, Dave says he has taken enough shots. Tikitta goes off for dinner with her squillionaire boyfriend. The donkey is asleep.

The new edition of **Look Good** hits the shops! For the front cover, I chose a photo of the donkey in a $2,000 hat that I took. Tikitta's boyfriend threatens to sue. Lots of publicity and the magazine sells out in double-quick time. Another success for me, I think!

Flaunt Your Best Aspects

You don't have to be stick-thin and 9 feet tall to be a model, you know. There's room for curvy people, and people of all ages, too. Models work everywhere, not just in couture shows.

Maybe one part of you is particularly lovely—your hands, eyes, or feet, for example. In that case, you could be an eye model for a glasses advertisement, a hand model for jewelry, or a foot model for shoes. Just look at these job ads I cut out to prove to you that everyone can model something.

Hand model wanted for *Witches Weekly*. Wrinkles, curly nails, and green skin preferred.

Foot model wanted for bunion advert. Needs to have awful feet with weird knobs on the side.

Back of the knee model needed for sock advert. Top half of the inner left ankle model also considered.

How To Be A Fashion Model

Lots of people say to me: "Lulu, what's the best way to succeed as a fashion model?" I've asked my friend Maggie from top model agency "Mugs r Us" to pass on some good advice.

Do

 1. Drink lots of water to make your skin look good.

2. Be patient while stylists do your hair and make your face up, over and over again.

 3. Sign up with a famous model agency like "Mugs r Us."

4. If you throw a tantrum, be careful not to mess up your hair.

 5. Practise the "miserable model look" for photographs. Try pouting and looking sulky, as if really bored.

6. Avoid having nose-mucus in close-up photos.

 7. Choose a wonderful, new, exotic name. I'll tell you a little secret. Super-model Tikitta used to be called Mavis Thringbottom.

Don't

 1. Eat a tray of cakes if you know you are going to be modeling a skimpy bikini.

 2. Sign up with some dumpy, useless model agency run from above a bus station by your cousin's friend's neighbor.

 3. Agree to model underwear in the Arctic.

 4. Agree to model wool coats in the Sahara.

Chapter 5

Makeover

People come to me for fashion advice day and night. They stop me at the oddest times, even when I'm out shopping or parking the car. Well, what can a fashion queen do? I usually give them a smile and a style tip and send them away happy, but if it's a full makeover they want, that's a different matter. I love makeovers! I immediately book them in for a Lulu Makeover Special, although I have to warn them there's a six-month waiting list. Of course, there are times when I'm called to an emergency makeover that just can't wait. Only the other night, I was chilling out in my penthouse, snuggled up with Snuffy and Lizzie on my pink zebra-striped sofa, when my pop star friend Sparkle appeared at my door in a panic. Sparkle is usually hot when it comes to style, but not this time. She was due to sing her latest hit on TV in two hours, but she'd just flown in from LA and lost all her luggage. I sprang into action.

First, the clothes. We pulled everything out of my drawers and closets until the place looked like it had been hit by a clothes hurricane. Then we got out all my shoes and tried on billion million costumes (well, at least twenty). Finally, I sat Sparkle in front of my super-deluxe "stage diva" mirror and went to work on her hair and makeup. That night, when she sang live on TV, her outfit started a whole set of new trends. You might even be wearing one now.

After my other friends heard about it, they all wanted the same fun, so I decided to throw a makeover party. Now, obviously for a party like that you need to provide hairbrushes, clothes, a mirror etc, etc. But there's one thing you absolutely must have—TACT! Luckily, as you already know, I am an expert at saying things gently. For instance, I would never say: "Your shoes are sooo wrong," or "I've wished for ages that you would change your hairdo."

No, no, no, NO! Listen to Lulu! I would say: "Try on this new shoe style, just for fun." or "Can I do your hair? Just for fun." My makeover party went fantastically well. My friends even wanted to give me a makeover. "Just for fun," they said. Mmm. Anyway, I asked everyone to come up with a makeover tip, a quick way to change a look, and here's what they all suggested:

If you have long hair put it up, or make it look bushy and "big" by using gel.

Use some hair mascara.

If you have short hair, use gel to spike it or give it a messy "just got up" look.

Try wearing a dress or skirt over your jeans, for a funky layered look.

Wear a short-sleeved top over a long-sleeved one for a groovy, street-style look.

Add different belts to a skirt.

To glam up a dress, wear it with a beaded sweater or a shawl. To make it look more relaxed, wear it with a denim jacket.

Play with your clothes, mixing and matching them in front of a mirror. That way, you may make an exciting new style all your own.

Swap an item of clothing with your friend for the day.

Try on different hats or bandannas.

DANGER!

Makeover Warning!

This page is painful for me to write, but I must, for your sake. You see, there's a pitfall with makeovers and even I fell into it recently. After I gave Sparkle and my other friends a makeover, I just got carried away. I'm afraid I got a dose of "makeover madness." I forgot my usual tact and started trying to change everyone I met.

First I told my neighbor that he badly needed to update himself past 1972. Ouch! Then I persuaded him to wear a leopard-print sarong skirt to work and he was nearly fired (I forgot he was a school principal). The next day I visited my parents and while my dad was asleep in his chair I spiked his hair with gel so he looked like Sonic the Hedgehog thirty years older. I forgot to tell him and he went to the grocery store, caught a glimpse of himself in a window, and fainted into a shopping cart. But I don't feel quite so guilty about my younger brother. He has no fashion sense at all because I inherited all there was in the family. While he was out of his apartment, I removed all his clothes and substituted an entire collection of new cutting-edge menswear in yellow linen with netting detail. He looked like a bag of bananas and was not happy.

I know, I know. I went too far. I can only say I was gripped by the madness.

My advice to you is to do makeovers on your friends, but always stay tactful and in control of yourself. Remember, it could be your turn for a makeover next...

Lulu's Photo Makeover

If you think you might catch makeover madness, I have the ideal answer, as usual. You'll get the chance to do celebrity makeovers just like I do. You needn't be tactful either. They'll be helpless. You can make them look any way you want! All you need is a glue stick, scissors, paper, and lots of old magazines.

Cut out photos of your favorite celebrities from magazines.

Stick the photos on a sheet of paper.

Now cut out hair and clothes from the magazines and try them on top of your celebrities to get the look you want.

You and your friends could do this with photos of each other.

Makeover wardrobe

Why not design a whole clothes collection for your celebrity? Cut out a whole figure, stick it on thick card, and cut around the card. Then make paper clothes that fit on to it with little shoulder or waist tabs.

Super Cool!

My Style Secrets

Do I have a perfect body shape? Of course! Do you even have to ask? Well... Since you're a friend, I will let you in on a little secret. I learned long ago how to disguise my tiny imperfections by dressing in the right clothes. I'll give you my tips if you promise to keep that piece of information very, very quiet.

If you want to look taller

☆ Wear all one color.

☆ Avoid big, baggy clothes. They will make you look shorter and wider.

☆ Wear vertical (up and down) stripes, not horizontal ones.

☆ Tuck shirts into pants to make your legs look longer.

If you want to look slimmer

☆ Wear all one color. Black or a dark color is very slimming.

☆ Try not to split your look at waist-height, with one color on top and another color on the bottom.

☆ Avoid shapeless baggy clothes. They will make you look bigger. Wear softly shaped clothes instead.

☆ Avoid clothes that are too tight.

☆ Don't wear horizontal stripes. They will make you look wider.

☆ Avoid pants with bulky pockets and pleats at the front. They will make you look bigger.

If you want to look less tall

☆ A long top will make your legs look shorter.

☆ Wear horizontal stripes, not vertical ones.

☆ If you dress all in one color you will look taller, so if you want to look shorter mix light and dark colors and shades.

What was that you said? What ARE my little imperfections exactly? Now THAT'S between me and my mirror!

My Secrets of Elegance

People often say how elegant I look, and that's because I have good posture. I stand tall, with my shoulders back, not hunched and stooping. It makes a big difference. If you don't believe me try my posture tips for yourself.

☆ Young ladies used to learn how to walk tall by balancing books on their heads and walking across a room. Try it. It's harder than you think!

☆ Stand sideways by a full-length mirror. Which part of your body is slouching? Maybe your shoulders are flopped over or your head is bent forward. Straighten up and see the difference.

☆ When you sit down in a chair, make sure your hips are far back, right against the back of the chair. If that feels uncomfortable, put a pillow behind you to keep your back straight when you sit.

I know you won't want to think about improving your posture all the time, but think about it occasionally, and especially if you are being photographed. Do you want to look like a slouching sadsack or a straight-up success? No contest, darlings!

PS: I've noticed that my celebrity friends often stand in a certain way to get their photo taken. They stand very slightly to the side, with one foot in front of the other. That way their shoulders naturally go back, and they look longer and leaner. Check it out next time you see stars photographed at a movie premiere.

what would you rather look like?!

Chapter 6

Glamor Girl

There's a time and a place when we fashion-lovers can shine like true stars. I'm talking about those occasions when only one look will do—glamor! When I go for glamor, I really go for it, and invariably as many cameras flash as there are sequins on my breathtaking party outfits. Only last week, I gracefully slipped out of my luxury limo on to a red carpet for an awards night, and the crowd went crazy. "Lulu lights up our lives," the headlines read the next day. I saw other stars shielding their eyes from the explosion of the flashbulbs, while crying into their silk hankies. They knew I'd stolen the show. I just can't help it when I'm glammed up, and I'm going to tell you how you can have the same effect.

To be a glamorous success, you need to think "theater." Imagine you are on stage, the star of a  show. What would you wear? You need something bold and exciting, with that "wow" factor that makes the audience focus on you. You might want to try some glitter that will be picked out by the lights. Ooh, just talking about it makes me want to try on my new skin-tight silver dress, wrap my feather boa around my neck, and party on down!

Silver, black, gold, red, and purple are all dramatic glamor colors. Shiny fabric, lace, and exciting clothes shapes also draw attention. Think Cinderella before midnight, think Hollywood, and, most of all, think Oscar Night. Think of the gasps, the "oohs" and "aaahs," as the stars go up to collect their awards in the most dazzling gowns on the planet. "And the winner is... Excuse me, Where DID you get that dress?"

OK, so maybe you won't be going to the Oscars, at least not yet, but if you don't get invited to many glamorous events, don't give up. Throw your own party and write on the invitation, "Dress as glamorous as you can." But make sure that no one looks more glamorous than you!

Look Chic on a Shoestring

Glamor is an expensive look, but there are ways to cheat and look a million dollars for almost nothing.

Save on sparklies

Look out for sparkly costume jewelry that costs very little but looks fun. You'd be surprised how much fake jewelry gets worn on big occasions... although not by me, of course...

Glitter girl

Use glitter body gel, glitter hair spray, and glitter makeup to add party shine.

Gloves a go-go

Buy a pair of long "evening" gloves and slip them on with a sleeveless dress. You'll immediately feel like a Hollywood screen goddess. I promise!

Oscar Countdown

I always get invited to the Oscars because fashion plays such an important part on the night, and they like to have a fashion icon like me there. All the stars dress their best, knowing their pictures are being sent around the world to TVs and magazines. They usually phone me beforehand, of course, asking for hints and tips on how to cope. I tell them that the three p's are the key—planning, preparation, and going to the toilet before you leave home. Here's my Oscar diary from last year:

Two days beforehand

I sift through all the dresses that top designers are begging me to borrow for the night. I have a mega trying-on session. It's hard to decide. Shall I choose a sweet Cinderella ballgown or a strapless black number? I text Sparkle for advice, and she says that the shiniest, glitteriest dress is the one to wear because it will light up everyone's TV sets.

One day beforehand ─────

At the beautician's nearly all day. I get my face, hands, eyebrows, legs, feet, and arms done. Glamor is hard work, but worth it.

The day of the Oscars ─────

I spend the morning at the hairdresser's, where I meet other stars having their split ends snipped. They beg me to tell them what I'm wearing, but I won't give away my secret. A glamorous outfit works best if it surprises people. I like to hear them gasp when I walk in.

Midday ─────

My jewelry arrives by armored car with eight security guards. The jewelry company insisted I borrow it all for free. Mmm. Well, all right then. If you insist. Time to start getting ready. Only six hours to go.

Evening ─────

The stretch limo is waiting outside. I'm ready to roll! Oh no, wait. I know I've forgotten something... Oh crime of all crimes! I nearly left my Versace scarf at home.

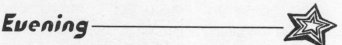

OSCAR NIGHT

It was a star-studded night, but one lady
sparkled the most. Goldie Bling reports

LULU WEARS
BEST DRESS

Fashion queen
Lulu stole the
show again with
her glitzy
entrance to the
Oscars last night.
Heartthrob stars
were seen to
swoon at her feet
and beg her for
dates, but she
said mysteriously
that her heart
belonged to
Snuffy. When
asked the secret
of her success,
she breathed one
word: "Glamor".

LULU WE ♥ U !!!

100

73

Know Your Glamor

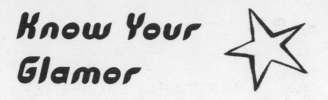

I'm a world authority on glamor. Perhaps THE world authority. Let's see how you shape up.

The answers are on the next page, but no peeking!

True or False?

1. Cher once wore an Oscar dress that looked like a see-through cobweb.

2. Lamé is a fabric made from goat hair.

3. Gold jewelry is more expensive than silver.

4. Most dresses and jewelry pieces are borrowed for Oscar night.

5. Silk is made by worms.

A or B?

6. The worst thing that could happen to you on Oscar night would be:
a) your dress splitting
b) your partner's pants splitting

7. Liz Hurley once wore a dress split up the sides and held together with:
a) safety pins b) tape

8. Which are a girl's best friend?
a) diamonds b) chocolate eclairs

9. For a glamor night, would you wear long hair a) up b) down?

10. With a long dress, would you wear a) flat shoes b) high heels?

Answers

1. **True** – Yes, Cher is famous for wearing either skimpy or weird clothes on Oscar night, but she's always glamorous.

2. **False** – Lamé is a great glamor fabric because it is made from silver or gold threads.

3. **True** – Gold is more expensive, but sometimes silver looks best. It depends on the outfit.

4. **True** – Yes, most of the outfits and jewelry pieces are lent by designers, to get publicity. Over $40 million worth of jewelry can be loaned to Oscar stars.

True – Yes, silkworms make silk, another good glamor fabric because it shimmers so prettily.

 a – If your dress split you could hold it together with safety pins (see Liz Hurley, number 7). But if your partner's pants split he would draw far too much attention from you.

 a – Safety pins, all the way up from bottom to top! She instantly became a star.

 a – This is a trick question, because it depends on the occasion. Technically, diamonds are correct, but chocolate eclairs can also be vital sometimes.

 a – If possible. How else are you going to show off your million-dollar earrings?

 b – So much more glamorous and they look great with evening dresses.

Glamor Clangers

There are a few nasty glamor traps you need to avoid. Just follow my lead and you'll be safe.

Glamor panic: You know you've got glamor panic when you agonize over what to wear to a big occasion until you can't even get out of your dressing gown. I have the answer, of course. If in doubt, wear black.

Losing it with shoes: Don't ruin a beautiful effect with grungy or frumpy shoes. Take a look in the mirror to make sure your shoes match your clothes before you go out.

Showing too much: Don't reveal more than you want to. Sometimes people wear such tiny dresses that they fall out of them by mistake. You know what I mean? Embarrassing or what?

Getting goosebumps: Take a shawl in case you get cold in a strapless party dress. If you shiver and turn blue, you won't enjoy yourself, and you'll look sad.

The rules of glamor

You can break most rules of fashion if you do it with style, but when it comes to glamorous party wear, there are some rules I advise you to stick to, and I am never wrong, darling.

Don't

Don't wear glamorous party clothes to the wrong occasion—for instance, a country walk or an appointment with the dentist. If you do, people will think, rightly, that you are crazy.

Don't overdo the jewelry and end up looking like a Christmas tree.

Don't be afraid of glamor. Obviously you won't be glamming-up all the time, but when you get the chance, try it. It's a wonderful feeling, like being Cinderella minus the ugly sisters and the midnight downer. Go for it, sweetie!

Chapter 7

Accessorize!

My collection of shoes, bags, hats, and jewelry has to be one of the biggest and best a girl ever had. In fact, my friend Sally, the TV presenter, did a whole program on them. I think they're planning to show it on prime time soon, so be ready. In the meantime, I persuaded her to let me include some of the program script in this chapter. I can't think why she was so surprised by my separate shoe, bag, and hat rooms. I am a fashion queen, after all. Imagine if I wore the same shoes all the time... it makes my toes curl in my peeptoe stilettos just to think about it!

Shoes

Never forget the effect your shoes can have. You can really let your look down with worn heels and grungy footwear. Get that shoe polish out, and

an old cleaning rag (or a pair of tired, old panties, see p89).

Hats ———————

I love hats because they are so artistic. There's a style for everyone, and they can be lots of fun. I'm not talking about boring baseball caps, though. I'm talking wide-brimmed, narrow-brimmed, tall, furry, crazily decorated... There are lots of possibilities, and you can be as original as you like.

Purses ———————

Purses can change your look in an instant, from fun and funky to elegant and expensive. Use them to look better than ever.

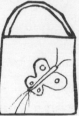

I love my accessories! Pass me my rhinestone cowboy hat and my monogrammed clutch bag. I'm going out to buy some more!

Lulu's Accessory Shop

I've laid out a few of my favorite accessories for you to have fun with, and I'll be watching you to see what kind of style you have. Imagine you have a little shift dress, plain colored, like the one I have out for you to see.

Now choose three accessories to go with it, and then add up your score to find out the truth about you and your outfit extras!

Fake Pearl Choker

Plain Shift Dress

Trendy trainers

Little leather shoulder bag

Original designer necklace

Chunky plastic bangle

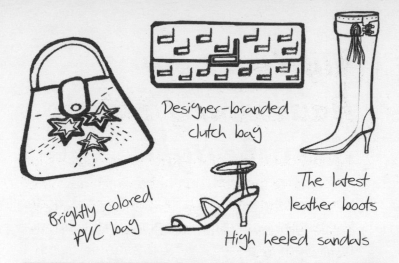

Designer-branded clutch bag

Brightly colored PVC bag

High heeled sandals

The latest leather boots

The Score Board

Brightly colored PVC bag	– Score 1
Little leather shoulder bag	– Score 2
Designer-branded clutch bag	– Score 3
Chunky plastic bangle	– Score 1
Fake pearl choker	– Score 2
Original designer necklace	– Score 3
Trendy trainers	– Score 1
High heeled sandals with straps	– Score 2
The latest leather boots	– Score 3

The truth about your accessories!

If you scored 3 or less, you have a funky, imaginative approach. Look for cool, street-style extras.

If you scored between 5 and 7, you go for elegant simplicity. Look for classically stylish stuff.

If you scored 8 or more, you love anything with a designer label. Keep up to date with new looks by browsing fashion magazines.

My TV Show
(with a little help from Sally)

Here is an excerpt from a TV show I've just made featuring my amazing collection of clothes and accessories. Sally, my TV presenter buddy, interviewed me at my apartment and in this section I showed her some of the accessories I've bought or been given. When the program comes out she wants to call it: "The Lulu Story." Yawn, yawn. I think it should be called: "Lulu—Fashion Superstar." Whatever you do, don't miss it, fashion fans!

Sally: I'm here in the stunning penthouse flat of Lulu, celebrity stylist, designer, model, fashion writer, and all-round style queen. Today she's going to show me her stunning collection of accessories. Lulu, I believe you have about three hundred pairs of shoes. Where do you keep them?

Lulu: Sally, darling. Lovely to see you and welcome to all my watching fans out there in fashion land. My shoes aren't here, sweetie. I have so many accessories, I need another apartment for them all. Come on, this way.

Sally: OK, we are now in Lulu's stunning "accessory" apartment. Let's look through the door marked "shoes." Goodness me! I've never seen so many pairs. Every color, every style... Lulu, which are your favorites?

Lulu: Oh, I change my mind all the time, but some pairs bring back fabulous memories. These strappy blue ones, for instance... I wore them to get my fourth award for: "Shoe Girl of the Year." I often get shoes as gifts. These gold trainers were given to me by the winning Rose Bowl football team for helping them out with a sock-length fashion crisis they had. This pair of red shoes was given to me by my film-star friend, Stella. She was in a space movie and I loaned her a silver bodysuit I had handy.

Sally: Now we move on to the hat room. Wow! They are all so beautiful!

Lulu: This is my latest one, made by Leonardo De Prism. It's fake fur decorated with fake mammoth bones, from his new "cavegirl" collection. It's going to be all the rage.

Sally: And here is your wonderful collection of purses. Do you have any advice for the viewers about purses?

Lulu: Think of them as precious pieces of art that you are carrying around. You wouldn't want to be seen with just any old junk, would you? Now Sally... Your shoes... Try on this new shoe style, just for fun. And your purse. Is that something you must have for your job? Here, try this hat.

Sally: Oh no. TV presenters don't wear hats.

Lulu: Great! You can start a new trend! Try this red one, and this feathered one, and how about this straw one?

Sally: No, Lulu. I don't think... Mmm, that one kind of suits me. May I try those shoes, too? And that purse...

(Program goes on for another two hours.)

Lulu's TV Appeal

This is the script from my last TV appeal. People were so moved. I had a lot of letters and someone even set up a home for abandoned hats.

"I am making this heartfelt appeal on behalf of shoes, hats, and purses everywhere. Please be kind to your accessories. Don't abandon them neglected and uncared for at the back of a dusty drawer, or worse, lying forgotten under your bed, while fashion passes them by, leaving them useless, sad little reminders of a forgotten trend."

"[sniff] Pass me a handkerchief would you, Sally?"

My campaign buttons

Take a purse for a night out

Shine your shoes

Hug your hats

All About Undies

No need to be shy with Lulu, darlings. I know ALL about what you wear underneath. Undies: thongs, boxer shorts, panties, corsets, bras, longjohns, t-shirts... They're all examples of that most important fashion item—your underwear. I know they aren't seen, but they help hold your shape and the shape of your clothes, so they have a vital fashion job. Here are my thoughts on undies:

Wear a thong if you are wearing really tight clothes. No VPL, thank you! (See my fashion disasters on page 12).

Get measured properly when it's time for you to wear a bra. Look in the back of a clothes catalog to see how it's done. I've noticed that bras are a bit like cars. Although there are already lots of different bra types, new ones are always being invented. In the future, there will probably be solar-heated, electronically adjusting ones. Hmm, I think I might patent that idea.

I've also noticed something about panties; they are a bit like human beings. However good they look to begin with, they always end up gray and baggy. If you have panties like that the kindest thing would be to let them retire and live a quiet, but useful life as a cleaning rag.

Wear the right underwear for the right occasion. If you want to avoid a frost-bitten rear, don't wear a thong on a winter sledging trip. Don't wear big, old, baggy panties when you go to a clothes shop with a communal shared dressing room. It would be like a horror movie scene, with everyone screaming.

THINGS TO DO

Ditch old panties and use them as dusting cloths, then rush out and buy nice new ones

Your Birthday Jewelry

I adore jewelry, of course. Did you know that each month has its own jewelry birthstone? I suggest you leave this list lying around when your birthday is coming up.

January
- **Garnet (a gorgeous dark red)**

February
- **Amethyst (fabulously purple)**

March
- **Aquamarine (the color of clear blue water)**

April
- **Diamond (lucky April)**

May
- **Emerald (rich green)**

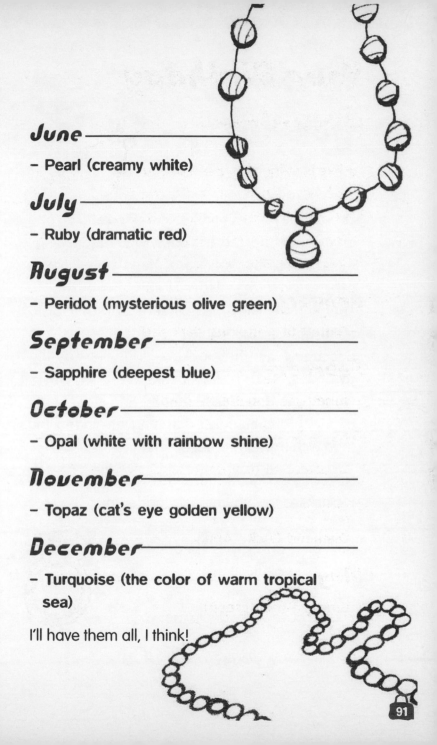

June

- Pearl (creamy white)

July

- Ruby (dramatic red)

August

- Peridot (mysterious olive green)

September

- Sapphire (deepest blue)

October

- Opal (white with rainbow shine)

November

- Topaz (cat's eye golden yellow)

December

- Turquoise (the color of warm tropical sea)

I'll have them all, I think!

Chapter 8

History just got hot

Do you sometimes find history lessons dull? I had an awful history teacher once, who made things much worse by wearing a green sweater with elbow patches. How was I expected to concentrate with that in front of me? Not to mention his pants, which I can't bring myself to describe fully; they looked as ancient as the pyramids. Also, history books are often dusty, which is no good for your nails. And what about all those archeologists scraping around in the mud with trowels? What do they look like?

Never fear, I have the answer to your history lesson yawns. Persuade your teacher to study the history of fashion. Not only is it soooo cool, it's fascinating, too. You'd never believe what some people have worn down the

ladies parasol 1800s

ages, and there are lots of surprises. Did you know that nobody wore pants for centuries, or panties, either? In ancient times, everyone wore tunics or skirts, and for underwear they wrapped loincloths around themselves. Awful VPL, I would think.

Corset from 1800s

The first-ever clothes were made from animal skins, which were very tough to start with. The simplest way to soften them was by chewing them, apparently, or bashing them with a big stone. What a lot of hard work to get some stinking bit of fur on you. Early humans even dressed in bark soaked in water—a kind of "tree tops" trend. Thank goodness somebody discovered weaving, or we'd all be walking around in this style-free stuff, smelling like a pile of compost or a wet dog.

As soon as decent clothes came along, the top people began to wear the finest ones, just like I do today. Kings and Queens wore expensive

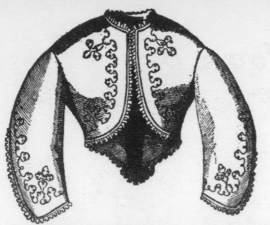

Jacket from 1800s

creations by their personal designers, woven with gold and encrusted with jewels. Standards were high. Make the King's hat too big, and you'd probably lose your head. As for the peasants, they wore...whatever. They could have used my book, which would have been written on a scroll, of course.

Modern designers still get plenty of inspiration from historical clothes, copying a shape perhaps, or a small detail. And with all of those centuries of style, I don't think archeologists or history teachers have any excuse for looking so bad.

Next time your teacher starts droning on about the past in a boring way, stand up proudly, wave my book, and ask this question:

"Yes, but what did they wear?"

Are You a Queen or a Peasant Girl?

If I could travel back in time, I think I'd do pretty well as a Queen— Cleopatra or Guinevere, perhaps. They had such  fab dresses. Where would you fit into history stylewise? Would you be a Queen in royal robes and jewels, or a pretty  peasant girl with flowing hair, a mop cap, and a flock of sheep to look after? Try my quiz to find out.

1. You see a large muddy puddle blocking your path. Do you:

a) Ask a handy knight to carry you over it.

b) Hitch up your skirts and wade through, laughing.

2. At a big castle feast, you would prefer to:

a) Flirt with the bravest knights.

b) Dance to the music of the minstrels.

3. If you had to make a historic speech, you would be better at:

a) Spurring your troops into battle.

b) Publicly denouncing a badly behaved lord of the manor.

4. You would prefer to own:

a) A velvet cloak of deepest midnight blue.

b) A finely embroidered petticoat as white as snow.

5. You would prefer:

a) A box of chocolates.

b) A bowl of strawberries and cream.

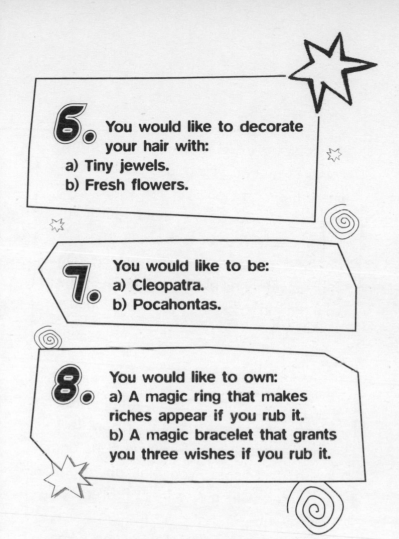

6. You would like to decorate your hair with:
a) Tiny jewels.
b) Fresh flowers.

7. You would like to be:
a) Cleopatra.
b) Pocahontas.

8. You would like to own:
a) A magic ring that makes riches appear if you rub it.
b) A magic bracelet that grants you three wishes if you rub it.

Add up the number of a's and b's you chose in my quiz. Then step into my time machine and prepare to travel wherever I send you!

Mostly a's

You belong on a throne with adoring courtiers around you and a closet full of finery. Bring on the velvet, the jewels, and the twenty pageboys to hold your train. Your majesty, you will look divine. The only downside is having to fight style wars with your next-door neighbor monarchs. Clothe your army in black and you should conquer them easily.

Mostly b's

You belong in the country, running free through the meadows in your bare feet. You would look best in simple skirts and embroidered tops, your hair down and decorated with a few fresh flowers. Be careful you don't step in the pig muck, though. There's a lot of it around when you're a peasant.

Through the Decades

The twentieth century was a very happening time for fashion. I was born, for example. Here's my run-through of those top fashion decades.

1900s

Women wore tight, tight corsets that made the waist look smaller but sometimes made it hard to breathe. Men and women always wore hats when they went outdoors. Women wore hats decorated with feathers and men sometimes wore stiff straw hats called boaters, along with impressive, tickly-looking mustaches.

1910s

Women wore skirts so narrow they were called "hobble" skirts. The first sneakers were worn, but only for sports. Anyone for tennis?

THINGS TO DO

Check out hobble skirts.
A good idea for next
season?

1920s

Drop-waisted dresses, bobbed hair, and lots of costume jewelry looked great for dancing to the hot new jazz music.

1930s

Think classic Hollywood glamor—starlets in slinky, flowing gowns with long gloves and men in detective hats and wide-shouldered overcoats. Here's lookin' at you, kid.

1940s

Wartime clothing looked like the military—being tailored to save on fabric, plain and simple. In the USA, jeans hit fashion town, and were worn rolled-up like pedal-pushers. Women began to wear pants much more, which some people thought was a terrible scandal.

THINGS TO DO

Ask Grandma.
Did she rock 'n' roll?

1950s

Rock 'n' roll burst on the scene. Watch the movie **Grease** to see this look—white t-shirts and leather jackets for boys, wide swinging skirts for girls, great for dancing the jive.

1960s

Fashion became completely cool. Miniskirts appeared. Boys grew their hair long. Style went "go-go" or "hippie chick." See the movie **Austin Powers** for this look. It's hard to imagine now, but 60s clothes caused a huge scandal at the time. Fashion really hit the headlines as a way of rebelling against old fuddy-duddy ideas.

1970s

The 70s started off with blue jeans bell-bottoms. But then a fashion earthquake called Punk changed everything. This style was aimed at shocking, with ripped trousers, leather, rubber, chains, and amazing spiked and colored hairstyles. At the other extreme, people began to wear a lot more exercise clothes, such as leotards and legwarmers.

1980s

Hair got bigger because hair mousse was invented. This was the age of power-dressing, with boldly designed, shoulder-padded power suits. There were also lots of leggings around for women, instead of pants.

1990s

Designer names got really popular, and were seen on sneakers, puffer jackets, baggy combat pants, and hooded coats. A lot of this style came from the streets of LA. Kids copied it when they saw rap bands wearing it on TV.

2000 +

It's up to you, fashion babes!

THINGS TO DO

Big hair is back. Buy crate of "mega-mousse."

What's coming back next week? Legwarmers, maybe? Be ready!

Wacky Fashion

Fashion sometimes goes to extremes. Check out these weird twentieth-century fads. Even I don't think I'll be trying these again.

In the 40s, there was a fashion for little girls to wear miniature outfits exactly matching their mother's clothes.

In the 60s, half a million paper dresses were sold in the USA. You could wear them for a week before they fell apart.

In 1964, the French designer Courréges suggested astronaut goggles as an accessory, while Paco Rabanne showed dresses made only of metal discs linked by chains.

In the 80s, designers came up with a white bridal jogging suit, complete with veil, and a ballgown made of see-through plastic.

In 1988, designer Franco Moschino showed his famous teddy bear dress, a black dress with toy teddy bears hanging around the neckline, and a matching teddy bear-covered hat.

Inventors, We Salute You
(and give you big hugs)

I have invented many trends, but I have to admit they don't always last. Take my green lipstick, for example. When I wore it, people thought I was ill and rushed me to the hospital. I had to go back to the drawing board on that one, but some people have changed the fashion world forever with their inventions.

Henry Seeley of New York invented the first electric iron in 1882. Before that, getting out creases was complicated, involving servants, hot stoves, flat irons. Frankly, I wouldn't have bothered.

The first zipper-type fastener

was devised in 1891, but was very unreliable, apparently. This sounds utterly disastrous. What if you were just meeting Queen Victoria when your pants fell down? In 1906, Gideon Sundback came to the rescue by inventing the modern zipper, and it was safe for the Queen to open her eyes again.

The first waterproof umbrella was made for King Louis XIII of France, and it sounds very stylish in oiled cloth trimmed with gold and silver lace. Quel cool.

In 1935, W. Carothers invented nylon from a chemical found in coal tar. It became all the rage, with nylon made into all kinds of clothing, from frilly pink nightgowns to those yucky nylon stretch tops that no one wears any more. Sorry, Carothers. Nylon is out.

THINGS TO DO

Must find out. is nylon in or out?? Suspect might be in?

Cleopatra, my total style heroine, was the first queen to use blusher, in around 50BC. She wowed boyfriend Antony by dabbing her cheeks with a mixture made from red clay.

Earlier, Queen Nefertiti was the first person to paint her nails red, around 1370BC. Only royals were allowed to do this at the time. Unfair!

Archduke Maximilian had the world's first diamond engagement ring made for his bride, Mary, in 1477. What a sweetheart.

The first person to wear high heels was Louis XIIII of France. He liked to dress up in a huge black wig, too. The man was fearless!

The Romans used a lot of eye makeup. For parties they wore it in black and gold—a daring look, but Caesar pulled it off, with the famous quote: "I came, I saw, I eyelined."

THINGS TO DO

Try out Cleo-style makeup at next photo shoot—so much chic potential!

Note to me:

Must try and invent something that will change fashion forever (other than myself, of course), make me (more) world famous, and guarantee my name goes down history!

What about teeth jewelry, or has that been done?

In 1850, Levi Strauss made the first pair of jeans for hard-working gold miners in California. Now that is a totally major fashion invention, don't you think?

In 1909, a lady wore the first swimsuit, which ended just above the knees. She got arrested, so you can imagine the effect of the first bikini, modelled in 1946. Calm down, judge! It's just a swimsuit with a few bits missing.

Oldies But Goodies

Everyone knows I love a new outfit, but there are lots of clever, chic ways to revamp old clothes, too. (Actually, I prefer to call them "vintage"—it sounds classier.) You can get yourself some great vintage bargains in second-hand stores. If you're really lucky, you might even find a garment with a designer label inside. A couture piece could sell for a lot of money at a collectible clothes auction.

The best way to learn about vintage clothes is to look at some fashion history books and websites. Valuable vintage couture names to look out for include Chanel, Dior, and St Laurent, plus famous 60s names such as Mary Quant. I have one of her original miniskirts, among the very first ever made. I wear it on special days with white go-go boots. Groovy gear!

Retro style is very "in," and a great way to get the clothes is to ask your adult relatives if you can hunt through their old things. They won't want to be seen again in their old 60s, 70s, and 80s clothes but on you it could look cool.

Ask your relatives what they used to wear in their teenage years. They might have some photos that a) could be hilarious, and b) could give you new ideas for your own designs. Anyway, adults love to talk about the fashions of their youth. Your problem will be shutting them up, so I advise you to stick to my 'I remember fashion' survey questions.

1) What was your favorite outfit as a child?

2) What were the most stylish clothes you had as a teenager?

3) Do you have any funky, old stuff that I could wear?

SERIOUS WARNING
RISK OF TOTAL PARENT MELTDOWN

NEVER ask an adult the following question:
"What do you think of the clothes worn by teenagers today?"

Vintage Chic

Recently I went to my local second-hand store to see if I could find any bargains to tell you about. After the shop-helpers had insisted I give them my autograph, they let me try on anything I liked and gave me these insider tips for you.

Horrors ─────────────────────────

Look at the inside armpits on a garment. If they aren't clean, the fabric is probably rotting by now. Don't buy it.

Check the collars and cuffs. If they are worn out don't bother. Wearing them will make you look worn yourself.

Look carefully for stains, rips, and moth holes.

Watch out for jewelry that has a cheap fake silver or gold surface that has rubbed off and looks ragged. Check for broken clasps, too.

Snap up ─────

Funky, retro jewelry. Stylish plastic pieces from the 60s and 70s are very collectible items now.

Clothes with definite period style—such as a swirly 70s shirt, a pop-group t-shirt from the 80s, or a little 60s minidress.

Look for clothes that are fun to wear, with something original about them.

Keep an eye on new fashion trends based on retro designs. As soon as you hear of a hot, new retro look, get down to those second-hand stores and start hunting.

Customize Your Stuff

I do wear clothes more than once, but people don't notice because I customize them with the latest hot fashion trend. I am a practical girl as well as being a fashion icon, you know. Why else would I be in such demand for celebrity makeovers and photo-shoot styling? Here are some of my customizing secrets, just for you.

Dye another day

You can dye things easily by using washing machine dye. Just ask for permission and read the instructions. Plain fabrics dye the best.

Tie dye, baby!

Tie string around and around a section of t-shirt, to make a bundle. Then dye it to get a freaky tie-dye effect.

Make a masterpiece

Buy a set of fabric pens or paints and settle
down with a plain white t-shirt to make
your very own work of art.

Iron-ons

Look in your local department store
for iron-on patches and
decorations to add to your clothes.
Denim looks really good with iron-ons.

Belt up

There are lots of great belts around. Wear a really
cool one to update an outfit.

Note to me:

Purple is going to be next
season's hottest color. Remember
to dye my t-shirts, my curtains,
Lizzie's cat blanket, and
Snuffy's dog-coat. Must send
purple dye to all my friends.

Are You A Fashion Original?

The hardest fashion look to pull off, but also the coolest, is to dress differently from everyone else yet with such style that they worship your original taste and want to copy you. Super-cool styles that are your own convey an impression of someone way ahead of the crowd. You need a very self-confident personality to strut your stuff separately like this, and to persuade everyone that you are a super-heated fashionista and not a fancy-dress act. Do you hear a fashion voice so strong you know that you must wear a vintage man's jacket, perhaps with a carefully placed Punk-style rip across the back, pink stilettos, and 70s tartan shorts?

If you think you can carry it off and you are certain that it is absolutely right for the moment, then go for it. You have a true fashion heart and we are sisters. If anyone laughs at you, send them to me.

Are You SERIOUS?

Here are some names given to fashion crazes from the twentieth century. Which ones are real vintage clothing and which ones are fake names I made up? (Naughty me!)

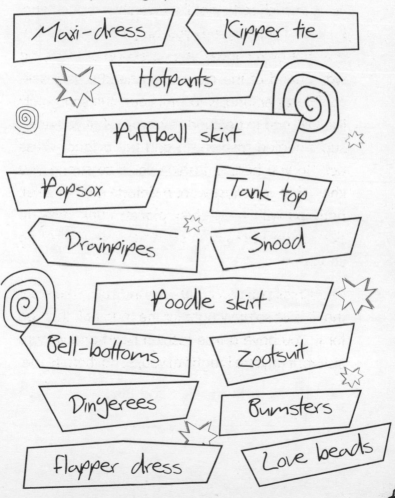

Maxi-dress

Kipper tie

Hotpants

Puffball skirt

Popsox

Tank top

Drainpipes

Snood

Poodle skirt

Bell-bottoms

Zootsuit

Dingerees

Bumsters

flapper dress

Love beads

Yes, Really!

Bell-bottoms: flaired sailor pants worn in the 60s and 70s.

Kipper tie: a very wide tie worn in the 60s.

Hotpants: shorts with bibs or braces, from the early 70s.

Puffball skirt: an 80s short skirt that puffed out and then gathered in at the hem.

Drainpipes: straight tight pants worn in the 70s and 80s.

flapper dress: **a 20s dress with a dropped waist.**

Love beads: **strings of small beads strung on wire or string. Very 1960s.**

Tank top: **60s sleeveless sweater with round neck.**

Snood: **a type of hair net/head scarf from the 40s.**

Popsox: **socks made of pantyhose fabric.**

Maxi-dress: **a long dress from the 60s and 70s.**

Poodle skirt: a wide swingy 50s skirt decorated with a poodle picture.

Bumsters: low-slung pants from the late 1990s.

Zootsuit: a man's suit with wide padded shoulders and narrow pants ankles (the kind you see on cartoon gangsters).

Dingerees: OK, I made that one up. But it's a cute name. I think I might design a pair and start a new trend.

Big Money, Baby

If you think my clothes collection is valuable (which of course, it is), take a look at these!

In 1962, Marilyn Monroe wore a long, beaded dress to sing "Happy Birthday" to US President Kennedy. The dress was sold at auction in 1999 for over a million dollars.

The world's most expensive fabric is vicuna, made from the wool of a Peruvian llama.

You can buy a bra for $15 million. Yes, million. It's encrusted with precious diamonds and rubies, and is delivered to you by armored truck.

THINGS TO DO

Look into burglar alarm for my wardrobe of priceless style.

Remember you can't buy style, but you can steal it!

Chapter 9

Lulu goes hi-tec (with hi-style)

In Japan, people are flocking to the stores to buy clothes that feed you vitamins while you wear them. Yes! It's absolutely true! The clothes are impregnated with vitamins, which gradually soak into your skin. They are supposed to help the person wearing them stay healthy and young-looking. This amazing fashion development has made me start thinking about what else we could add to our twenty-first-century clothing.

How about clothes that tan you as you wear them, so you don't let those damaging sun rays near you? If you ever felt sick, you could put on clothes with medicine in them that gradually soaks into your skin. I think this idea could be a big success and I have already sketched a pair of headache pants and an upset-stomach-hat.

I'm also mulling over the idea of exam review pajamas. These would gently play a recording of test answers through tiny speakers on the buttons, while you slept peacefully through the night. When you woke up, you would know everything.

I know! I have just thought of the perfect invention! It's a little bit like the paper dress idea in the 1960s, but much cooler for the modern age.

I can see it now. All I need to do is produce a range of clothes programmed to fall apart as soon as they go out of style! Each outfit would be fitted with a microchip electronically linked to my computer. As soon as I send a signal, the outfits would become unwearable (I'd give you an hour's warning so you could change before your clothes crumbled into a pile of dust). What a breakthrough! With my expertise, you need never be dressed unfashionably again. In a way, I will have saved the world—from badly coordinated separates, anyway.

THINGS TO DO

find a scientist ASAP!

The future starts here!

Dream On, Fashion Fans

Darlings! It's nearly time to leave. I must go to another clothes show, appear on another TV program and answer some more emergency style-calls from celebrities. (Her majesty Queen Elizabeth called from the UK again. She wants to try the goth look.) And you, my fashion fans, must go back to your closets and dress for success!

I've given you some tips for fashion style, but of course you can do your own thing. You don't need to listen to me all the time. Fashion is partly about creativity, after all. Just promise me you won't ever ignore the effect your clothes are having on you and the people who see you.

Actually, wait a minute. I've just reread that last part and I don't want you to run away with the wrong idea. Before you go crazy and wear whatever you like, there are a few things I insist on. If I ruled the world (and I suppose someone will ask me to one day), I'd have a few fashion laws, I can tell you...

No. I take that back. I sound like a fashion-fanatic, forcing dress laws on people who might not even be interested in clothes much. (A chilling thought, I know.)

Hmm. Well, maybe just one fashion law:

Nobody is ever to wear smelly clothes.

There. I think that's fair on everyone, don't you?

Oh, and no check golf pants... And no pink ties on men... And no football clothes at formal occasions... And no old housecoats with frayed edges... And no dodgy socks. I think that's all— for now.

THINGS TO DO

Confiscate Daddy's check golf pants, pink ties, dodgy socks, etc. He can be so embarrassing!

Lulu's Crystal Ball

Let's look far into the future now, fashion lovers. I fully intend to be there, maybe as a clone or a hologram. One thing's for sure: I'll be wearing whatever's in fashion. Here are my predictions for cool clothes in the year 3000.

Spacesuits will be the new combat pants. Everyone will be wearing them. I'd like one with cowboy fringe, Elvis-style rhinestones, and maybe a fake fur trim for those chilly spacewalks.

Clothes will be programmed to change color and shape as we wish. Bliss! That means no more problems running into someone wearing the same outfit, and if a trend drops out of style, we will simply tell our clothes to alter themselves.

Fashion shows will feature holograms of funky, famous people from history, such as Cleopatra or

Louis XIIII, wearing the new clothes.

There will be a new word: luluicious, meaning "well-dressed and gorgeous."

My accessory collection will be shown at the Lulu International Museum of Fashion Cool.

Men will become more and more interested in fashion until they go back to wearing embroidered frockcoats, powdered wigs, and breeches. They will look luluicious!

My dog Snuffy and my cat Lizzie will be clones or holograms, too, and will have their own dinky little spacesuits.

Be happy,
fashion fans.
Dress well!
Love and kisses
from

Lulu B